I0162686

Utopia, Limited

Utopia, Limited
Arthur Sullivan
and W.S. Gilbert

MINT EDITIONS

Utopia, Limited was first published in 1893.

This edition published by Mint Editions 2021.

ISBN 9781513281391 | E-ISBN 9781513286419

Published by Mint Editions®

MINT
EDITIONS

minteditionbooks.com

Publishing Director: Jennifer Newens
Design & Production: Rachel Lopez Metzger
Project Manager: Micaela Clark
Typesetting: Westchester Publishing Services

DRAMATIS PERSONAE

King Paramount, the First (King of Utopia)
Scaphio and Phantis (Judges of the Utopian Supreme Court)
Tarara (The Public Exploder)
Calynx (The Utopian Vice-Chamberlain)

Imported Flowers of Progress:

Lord Dramaleigh (a British Lord Chamberlain)
Captain Fitzbattleaxe (First Life Guards)
Captain Sir Edward Corcoran, K.C.B. (of the Royal Navy)
Mr. Goldbury (a company promoter; afterwards Comptroller of
    the Utopian Household)
Sir Bailey Barre, Q.C., M.P.
Mr. Blushington (of the County Council)

The Princess Zara (eldest daughter of King Paramount)
The Princesses Nekaya and Kalyba (her Younger Sisters)
The Lady Sophy (their English Gouvernante)

Utopian Maidens:
    Salata
    Melene
    Phylla

Act I
A Utopian Palm Grove

Act II
Throne Room in King Paramount's Palace

Act I

OPENING CHORUS.

In lazy languor—motionless,
We lie and dream of nothingness;
   For visions come
   From Poppydom
      Direct at our command:
Or, delicate alternative,
In open idleness we live,
   With lyre and lute
   And silver flute,
      The life of Lazyland.

SOLO—Phylla.

The song of birds
   In ivied towers;
      The rippling play
      Of waterway;
The lowing herds;
   The breath of flowers;
      The languid loves
      Of turtle doves—
These simply joys are all at hand
Upon thy shores, O Lazyland!

(*Enter Calynx*)

CALYNX: Good news! Great news! His Majesty's eldest
   daughter, Princess Zara, who left our shores five years since
   to go to England—the greatest, the most powerful, the wisest
   country in the world—has taken a high degree at Girton, and
   is on her way home again, having achieved a complete mastery
   over all the elements that have tended to raise that glorious
   country to her present pre-eminent position among civilized
   nations!

SALATA: Then in a few months Utopia may hope to be completely
   Anglicized?

CALYNX: Absolutely and without a doubt.

MELENE: (*lazily*) We are very well as we are. Life without a care—every want supplied by a kind and fatherly monarch, who, despot though he be, has no other thought than to make his people happy—what have we to gain by the great change that is in store for us?

SALATA: What have we to gain? English institutions, English tastes, and oh, English fashions!

CALYNX: England has made herself what she is because, in that favored land, every one has to think for himself. Here we have no need to think, because our monarch anticipates all our wants, and our political opinions are formed for us by the journals to which we subscribe. Oh, think how much more brilliant this dialogue would have been, if we had been accustomed to exercise our reflective powers! They say that in England the conversation of the very meanest is a coruscation of impromptu epigram!

(*Enter Tarara in a great rage*)

TARARA: Lalabalele talala! Callabale lalabalica falahle!

CALYNX: (*horrified*) Stop—stop, I beg! (*All the ladies close their ears*)

TARARA: Callamalala galalate! Caritalla lalabalee kallalale poo!

LADIES: Oh, stop him! stop him!

CALYNX: My lord, I'm surprised at you. Are you not aware that His Majesty, in his despotic acquiescence with the emphatic wish of his people, has ordered that the Utopian language shall be banished from his court, and that all communications shall henceforward be made in the English tongue?

TARARA: Yes, I'm perfectly aware of it, although—(*suddenly presenting an explosive "cracker"*). Stop—allow me.

CALYNX: (*pulls it*). Now, what's that for?

TARARA: Why, I've recently been appointed Public Exploder to His Majesty, and as I'm constitutionally nervous, I must accustom myself by degrees to the startling nature of my duties. Thank you. I was about to say that although, as Public Exploder, I am next in succession to the throne, I neverthless do my best to fall in with the royal decree. But when I am overmastered by an indignant sense of overwhelming wrong, as I am now, I slip into my native tongue without knowing it. I am told that in the language of that great and pure nation, strong expressions do not exist, consequently when I want to let off steam I have no alternative but to say, "Lalabalele molola lililah kallalale poo!"

ARTHUR SULLIVAN AND W.S. GILBERT

CALYNX: But what is your grievance?

TARARA: This—by our Constitution we are governed by a Despot who, although in theory absolute—is, in practice, nothing of the kind— being watched day and night by two Wise Men whose duty it is, on his very first lapse from political or social propriety, to denounce him to me, the Public Exploder, and it then becomes my duty to blow up His Majesty with dynamite—allow me. (*Presenting a cracker which Calynx pulls*) Thank you—and, as some compensation to my wounded feelings, I reign in his stead.

CALYNX: Yes. After many unhappy experiments in the direction of an ideal Republic, it was found that what may be described as a Despotism tempered by Dynamite provides, on the whole, the most satisfactory description of ruler—an autocrat who dares not abuse his autocratic power.

TARARA: That's the theory—but in practice, how does it act? Now, do you ever happen to see the Palace Peeper? (*producing a "Society" paper*).

CALYNX: Never even heard of the journal.

TARARA: I'm not surprised, because His Majesty's agents always buy up the whole edition; but I have an aunt in the publishing department, and she has supplied me with a copy. Well, it actually teems with circumstantially convincing details of the King's abominable immoralities! If this high-class journal may be believed, His Majesty is one of the most Heliogabalian profligates that ever disgraced an autocratic throne! And do these Wise Men denounce him to me? Not a bit of it! They wink at his immoralities! Under the circumstances I really think I am justified in exclaiming "Lalabelele molola lililah kalabalale poo!" (*All horrified*) I don't care—the occasion demands it. (*Exit Tarara*)

(*March. Enter Guard, escorting Scaphio and Phantis*)

CHORUS.

O make way for the Wise Men!
  They are the prizemen—
 Double-first in the world's university!
For though lovely this island
  (Which is my land),
 She has no one to match them in her city.

They're the pride of Utopia—
    Cornucopia
  Is each his mental fertility.
O they make no blunder,
    And no wonder,
  For they're triumphs of infallibility.

DUET—Scaphio and Phantis.

In every mental lore
  (The statement smacks of vanity)
We claim to rank before
  The wisest of humanity.
As gifts of head and heart
  We wasted on "utility,"
We're "cast" to play a part
  Of great responsibility.

Our duty is to spy
  Upon our King's illicites,
And keep a watchful eye
  On all his eccentricities.
If ever a trick he tries
  That savours of rascality,
At our decree he dies
  Without the least formality.

We fear no rude rebuff,
  Or newspaper publicity;
Our word is quite enough,
  The rest is electricity.
A pound of dynamite
  Explodes in his auriculars;
It's not a pleasant sight—
  We'll spare you the particulars.

Its force all men confess,
  The King needs no admonishing—
We may say its success

Is something quite astonishing.
Our despot it imbues
    With virtues quite delectable,
He minds his P's and Q's,—
    And keeps himself respectable.

Of a tyrant polite
He's paragon quite.
He's as modest and mild
In his ways as a child;
And no one ever met
With an autocrat yet,
So delightfully bland
To the least in the land!

    So make way for the wise men, etc.
(*Exeunt all but Scaphio and Phantis. Phantis is pensive*)

SCAPHIO: Phantis, you are not in your customary exuberant spirits. What is wrong?

PHANTIS: Scaphio, I think you once told me that you have never loved?

SCAPHIO: Never! I have often marvelled at the fairy influence which weaves its rosy web about the faculties of the greatest and wisest of our race; but I thank Heaven I have never been subjected to its singular fascination. For, oh, Phantis! there is that within me that tells me that when my time does come, the convulsion will be tremendous! When I love, it will be with the accumulated fervour of sixty-six years! But I have an ideal—a semi-transparent Being, filled with an inorganic pink jelly—and I have never yet seen the woman who approaches within measurable distance of it. All are opaque—opaque—opaque!

PHANTIS: Keep that ideal firmly before you, and love not until you find her. Though but fifty-five, I am an old campaigner in the battle-fields of Love; and, believe me, it is better to be as you are, heart-free and happy, than as I am—eternally racked with doubting agonies! Scaphio, the Princess Zara returns from England today!

SCAPHIO: My poor boy, I see it all.

PHANTIS: Oh! Scaphio, she is so beautiful. Ah! you smile, for you have never seen her. She sailed for England three months before you took office.

Scaphio: Now tell me, is your affection requited?

Phantis: I do not know—I am not sure. Sometimes I think it is, and then come these torturing doubts! I feel sure that she does not regard me with absolute indifference, for she could never look at me without having to go to bed with a sick headache.

Scaphio: That is surely something. Come, take heart, boy! you are young and beautiful. What more could maiden want?

Phantis: Ah! Scaphio, remember she returns from a land where every youth is as a young Greek god, and where such beauty as I can boast is seen at every turn.

Scaphio: Be of good cheer! Marry her, boy, if so your fancy wills, and be sure that love will come.

Phantis: (*overjoyed*) Then you will assist me in this?

Scaphio: Why, surely! Silly one, what have you to fear? We have but to say the word, and her father must consent. Is he not our very slave? Come, take heart. I cannot bear to see you sad.

Phantis: Now I may hope, indeed! Scaphio, you have placed me on the very pinnacle of human joy!

Duet—Scaphio and Phantis.

Scaphio: Let all your doubts take wing—
    Our influence is great.
  If Paramount our King
    Presume to hesitate
      Put on the screw,
        And caution him
      That he will rue
        Disaster grim
      That must ensue
        To life and limb,
      Should he pooh-pooh
        This harmless whim.

Both: This harmless whim—this harmless whim,
    It is as I/you say, a harmless whim.

Phantis: (*dancing*) Observe this dance
        Which I employ

When I, by chance
Go mad with joy.
What sentiment
Does this express?

(*Phantis continues his dance while Scaphio vainly endeavors to discover its meaning*)

Supreme content
And happiness!

BOTH: Of course it does! Of course it does!
Supreme content and happiness.

PHANTIS: Your friendly aid conferred,
I need no longer pine.
I've but to speak the word,
And lo, the maid is mine!
I do not choose
To be denied.
Or wish to lose
A lovely bride—
If to refuse
The King decide,
The royal shoes
Then woe betide!

BOTH: Then woe betide—then woe betide!
The Royal shoes then woe betide!

SCAPHIO: (*Dancing*) This step to use
I condescend
Whene'er I choose
To serve a friend.
What it implies
Now try to guess;

(*Scaphio continues his dance while Phantis is vainly endeavouring to discover its meaning*)

It typifies
Unselfishness!

BOTH: (*Dancing*) Of course it does! Of course it does!
It typifies unselfishness.

(*Exeunt Scaphio and Phantis*)

March. Enter King Paramount, attended by guards and nobles, and preceded by girls dancing before him.

Chorus.

Quaff the nectar—cull the roses—
    Gather fruit and flowers in plenty!
For our king no longer poses—
    Sing the songs of far niente!
Wake the lute that sets us lilting,
    Dance a welcome to each comer;
Day by day our year is wilting—
    Sing the sunny songs of summer!
        La, la, la, la!

Solo—King.

A King of autocratic power we—
    A despot whose tyrannic will is law—
Whose rule is paramount o'er land and sea,
    A presence of unutterable awe!
But though the awe that I inspire
Must shrivel with imperial fire
    All foes whom it may chance to touch,
To judge by what I see and hear,
It does not seem to interfere
    With popular enjoyment, much.
Chorus: No, no—it does not interfere
    With our enjoyment much.

Stupendous when we rouse ourselves to strike,
    Resistless when our tyrant thunder peals,
We often wonder what obstruction's like,
    And how a contradicted monarch feels.
But as it is our Royal whim
Our Royal sails to set and trim
    To suit whatever wind may blow—
What buffets contradiction deals
And how a thwarted monarch feels
    We probably will never know.
Chorus: No, no—what thwarted monarch feels,
    You'll never, never know.

RECITATIVE—King.

My subjects all, it is your with emphatic
That all Utopia shall henceforth be modelled
Upon that glorious country called Great Britain—
To which some add—but others do not—Ireland.
CHORUS: It is!
KING: That being so, as you insist upon it,
     We have arranged that our two younger daughters
     Who have been "finished" by an English Lady—
(*tenderly*) A grave and good and gracious English Lady—
     Shall daily be exhibited in public,
     That all may learn what, from the English standpoint,
     Is looked upon as maidenly perfection!
     Come hither, daughters!
(*Enter Nekaya and Kalyba. They are twins, about fifteen years old; they are
very modest and demure in their appearance, dress and manner. They stand
with their hands folded and their eyes cast down*)

CHORUS.

How fair! how modest! how discreet!
     How bashfully demure!
          See how they blush, as they've been taught,
          At this publicity unsought!
How English and how pure!

DUET—Nekaya and Kalyba.

BOTH: Although of native maids the cream,
     We're brought up on the English scheme—
          The best of all
          For great and small
               Who modesty adore.
NEK.: For English girls are good as gold,
     Extremely modest (*so we're told*)
     Demurely coy—divinely cold—
          And that we are—and more.
KAL.: To please papa, who argues thus—

All girls should mould themselves on us
  Because we are
  By furlongs far
    The best of the bunch,
  We show ourselves to loud applause
  From ten to four without a pause—
NEK.: Which is an awkward time because
    It cuts into our lunch.
BOTH: Oh maids of high and low degree,
  Whose social code is rather free,
  Please look at us and you will see
  What good young ladies ought to be!
NEK.: And as we stand, like clockwork toys,
  A lecturer whom papa employs
    Proceeds to praise
    Our modest ways
      And guileless character—
KAL.: Our well-known blush—our downcast eyes—
  Our famous look of mild surprise.
NEK.: (*Which competition still defies*)—
      Our celebrated "Sir!!!"
KAL.: Then all the crowd take down our looks
  In pocket memorandum books.
    To diagnose
    Our modest pose
      The Kodaks do their best:
NEK.: If evidence you would possess
  Of what is maiden bashfulness
  You need only a button press—
KAL.: And we will do the rest.
Enter Lady Sophy—an English lady of mature years and extreme gravity of demeanour and dress. She carries a lecturer's wand in her hand. She is led on by the King, who expresses great regard and admiration for her.

RECITATIVE—Lady Sophy.

This morning we propose to illustrate
A course of maiden courtship, from the start
To the triumphant matrimonial finish.

(Through the following song the two Princesses illustrate in gesture the description given by Lady Sophy)

Song—Lady Sophy.

Bold-faced ranger
(*Perfect stranger*)
Meets two well-behaved young ladies.
He's attractive,
Young and active—
Each a little bit afraid is.
Youth advances,
At his glances
To their danger they awaken;
They repel him
As they tell him
He is very much mistaken.
Though they speak to him politely,
Please observe they're sneering slightly,
Just to show he's acting vainly.
This is Virtue saying plainly
"Go away, young bachelor,
We are not what you take us for!"
When addressed impertinently,
English ladies answer gently,
"Go away, young bachelor,
We are not what you take us for!"

As he gazes,
Hat he raises,
Enters into conversation.
Makes excuses—
This produces
Interesting agitation.
He, with daring,
Undespairing,
Give his card—his rank discloses
Little heeding
This proceeding,

They turn up their little noses.
Pray observe this lesson vital—
When a man of rank and title
His position first discloses,
Always cock your little noses.
　　When at home, let all the class
　　Try this in the looking glass.
English girls of well bred notions,
Shun all unrehearsed emotions.
　　English girls of highest class
　　Practice them before the glass.

　　His intentions
　　Then he mentions.
Something definite to go on—
　　Makes recitals
　　Of his titles,
Hints at settlements, and so on.
　　Smiling sweetly,
　　They, discreetly,
Ask for further evidences:
　　Thus invited,
　　He, delighted,
Gives the usual references:
This is business. Each is fluttered
When the offer's fairly uttered.
"Which of them has his affection?"
He declines to make selection.
　　Do they quarrel for his dross?
　　Not a bit of it—they toss!
Please observe this cogent moral—
English ladies never quarrel.
　　When a doubt they come across,
　　English ladies always toss.

RECITATIVE—Lady Sophy.

The lecture's ended. In ten minute's space
'Twill be repeated in the market-place!

　　　　　　ARTHUR SULLIVAN AND W.S. GILBERT

(*Exit Lady Sophy, followed by Nekaya and Kalyba*)

CHORUS: Quaff the nectar—cull the roses—
    Bashful girls will soon be plenty!
  Maid who thus at fifteen poses
    Ought to be divine at twenty!

(*Exeunt all but* KING)

KING: I requested Scaphio and Phantis to be so good as to favor me with an audience this morning. (*Enter* SCAPHIO *and* PHANTIS) Oh, here they are!

SCAPHIO: Your Majesty wished to speak with us, I believe. You—you needn't keep your crown on, on our account, you know.

KING: I beg your pardon. (*Removes it*) I always forget that! Odd, the notion of a King not being allowed to wear one of his own crowns in the presence of two of his own subjects.

PHANTIS: Yes—bizarre, is it not?

KING: Most quaint. But then it's a quaint world.

PHANTIS: Teems with quiet fun. I often think what a lucky thing it is that you are blessed with such a keen sense of humor!

KING: Do you know, I find it invaluable. Do what I will, I cannot help looking at the humorous side of things—for, properly considered, everything has its humorous side—even the Palace Peeper (*producing it*). See here—"Another Royal Scandal," by Junius Junior. "How long is this to last?" by Senex Senior. "Ribald Royalty," by Mercury Major. "Where is the Public Exploder?" by Mephistopheles Minor. When I reflect that all these outrageous attacks on my morality are written by me, at your command—well, it's one of the funniest things that have come within the scope of my experience.

SCAPHIO: Besides, apart from that, they have a quiet humor of their own which is simply irresistible.

KING: (*gratified*) Not bad, I think. Biting, trenchant sarcasm—the rapier, not the bludgeon—that's my line. But then it's so easy—I'm such a good subject—a bad King but a good Subject—ha! ha!—a capital heading for next week's leading article! (*makes a note*) And then the stinging little paragraphs about our Royal goings-on with our Royal Second Housemaid—delicately sub-acid, are they not?

SCAPHIO: My dear King, in that kind of thing no one can hold a candle to you.

PHANTIS: But the crowning joke is the Comic Opera you've written for us—"King Tuppence, or A Good Deal Less than Half a Sovereign"—in which the celebrated English tenor, Mr. Wilkinson, burlesques your personal appearance and gives grotesque imitations of your Royal peculiarities. It's immense!

KING: Ye—es—That's what I wanted to speak to you about. Now I've not the least doubt but that even that has its humorous side too—if one could only see it. As a rule I'm pretty quick at detecting latent humor—but I confess I do not quite see where it comes in, in this particular instance. It's so horribly personal!

SCAPHIO: Personal? Yes, of course it's personal—but consider the antithetical humor of the situation.

KING: Yes. I—I don't think I've quite grasped that.

SCAPHIO: No? You surprise me. Why, consider. During the day thousands tremble at your frown, during the night (*from 8 to 11*) thousands roar at it. During the day your most arbitrary pronouncements are received by your subjects with abject submission—during the night, they shout with joy at your most terrible decrees. It's not every monarch who enjoys the privilege of undoing by night all the despotic absurdities he's committed during the day.

KING: Of course! Now I see it! Thank you very much. I was sure it had its humorous side, and it was very dull of me not to have seen it before. But, as I said just now, it's a quaint world.

PHANTIS: Teems with quiet fun.

KING: Yes. Properly considered, what a farce life is, to be sure!

SONG—King.

First you're born—and I'll be bound you
Find a dozen strangers round you.
"Hallo," cries the new-born baby,
"Where's my parents? which may they be?"
    Awkward silence—no reply—
    Puzzled baby wonders why!
Father rises, bows politely—
Mother smiles (*but not too brightly*)—

Doctor mumbles like a dumb thing—
Nurse is busy mixing something—
    Every symptom tends to show
    You're decidedly de trop—
ALL: Ho! ho! ho! ho! ho! ho! ho! ho!
        Time's teetotum,
          If you spin it,
        Gives it quotum
          Once a minute.
        I'll go bail
        You hit the nail,
        And if you fail,
          The deuce is in it!
KING: You grow up and you discover
    What it is to be a lover.
    Some young lady is selected—
    Poor, perhaps, but well-connected.
        Whom you hail (*for Love is blind*)
        As the Queen of fairy kind.
    Though she's plain—perhaps unsightly,
    Makes her face up—laces tightly,
    In her form your fancy traces
    All the gifts of all the graces.
        Rivals none the maiden woo,
        So you take her and she takes you.
ALL: Ho! ho! ho! ho! ho! ho! ho! ho!
        Joke beginning,
          Never ceases
        Till your inning
          Time releases,
    On your way
    You blindly stray,
    And day by day
        The joke increases!
KING: Ten years later—Time progresses—
    Sours your temper—thins your tresses;
    Fancy, then, her chain relaxes;
    Rates are facts and so are taxes.
        Fairy Queen's no longer young—

Fairy Queen has got a tongue.
Twins have probably intruded—
Quite unbidden—just as you did—
They're a source of care and trouble—
Just as you were—only double.
 Comes at last the final stroke—
 Time has had its little joke!
ALL: Ho! ho! ho! ho! ho! ho! ho! ho!
 Daily driven
  (*Wife as drover*)
 Ill you've thriven—
  Ne'er in clover;
 Lastly, when
 Three-score and ten
 (*And not till then*),
  The joke is over!
 Ho! ho! ho! ho! ho! ho! ho! ho!
 Then—and then
  The joke is over!
(*Exeunt Scaphio and Phantis*)

KING: (*putting on his crown again*) It's all very well. I always like to look on the humorous side of things; but I do not think I ought to be required to write libels on my own moral character. Naturally, I see the joke of it—anybody would—but Zara's coming home today; she's no longer a child, and I confess I should not like her to see my Opera—though it's uncommonly well written; and I should be sorry if the Palace Peeper got into her hands—though it's certainly smart—very smart indeed. It is almost a pity that I have to buy up the whole edition, because it's really too good to be lost. And Lady Sophy—that blameless type of perfect womanhood! Great Heavens, what would she say if the Second Housemaid business happened to meet her pure blue eye! (*Enter Lady Sophy*)

LADY S.: My monarch is soliloquizing. I will withdraw. (*going*)

KING: No—pray don't go. Now I'll give you fifty chances, and you won't guess whom I was thinking of.

LADY S.: Alas, sir, I know too well. Ah! King, it's an old, old story, and I'm wellnigh weary of it! Be warned in time—from my heart I pity you, but I am not for you! (*going*)

KING: But hear what I have to say.

LADY S.: It is useless. Listen. In the course of a long and adventurous career in the principal European Courts, it has been revealed to me that I unconsciously exercise a weird and supernatural fascination over all Crowned Heads. So irresistible is this singular property, that there is not a European Monarch who has not implored me, with tears in his eyes, to quit his kingdom, and take my fatal charms elsewhere. As time was getting on it occurred to me that by descending several pegs in the scale of Respectability I might qualify your Majesty for my hand. Actuated by this humane motive and happening to possess Respectability enough for Six, I consented to confer Respectability enough for Four upon your two younger daughters—but although I have, alas, only Respectability enough for Two left, there is still, as I gather from the public press of this country (*producing the Palace Peeper*), a considerable balance in my favor.

KING: (*aside*) Damn! (*aloud*) May I ask how you came by this?

LADY S.: It was handed to me by the officer who holds the position of Public Exploder to your Imperial Majesty.

KING: And surely, Lady Sophy, surely you are not so unjust as to place any faith in the irresponsible gabble of the Society press!

LADY S.: (*referring to paper*) I read on the authority of Senex Senior that your Majesty was seen dancing with your Second Housemaid on the Oriental Platform of the Tivoli Gardens. That is untrue?

KING: Absolutely. Our Second Housemaid has only one leg.

LADY S.: (*suspiciously*) How do you know that?

KING: Common report. I give you my honor.

LADY S.: It may be so. I further read—and the statement is vouched for by no less an authority that Mephistopheles Minor—that your Majesty indulges in a bath of hot rum-punch every morning. I trust I do not lay myself open to the charge of displaying an indelicate curiosity as to the mysteries of the royal dressing-room when I ask if there is any foundation for this statement?

KING: None whatever. When our medical adviser exhibits rum-punch it is as a draught, not as a fomentation. As to our bath, our valet plays the garden hose upon us every morning.

LADY S.: (*shocked*) Oh, pray—pray spare me these unseemly details.
   Well, you are a Despot—have you taken steps to slay this scribbler?
KING: Well, no—I have not gone so far as that. After all, it's the poor
   devil's living, you know.
LADY S.: It is the poor devil's living that surprises me. If this man lies,
   there is no recognized punishment that is sufficiently terrible for him.
KING: That's precisely it. I—I am waiting until a punishment is
   discovered that will exactly meet the enormity of the case. I am
   in constant communication with the Mikado of Japan, who is a
   leading authority on such points; and, moreover, I have the ground
   plans and sectional elevations of several capital punishments in
   my desk at this moment. Oh, Lady Sophy, as you are powerful, be
   merciful!

DUET—King and Lady Sophy.

KING: Subjected to your heavenly gaze
         (*Poetical phrase*),
      My brain is turned completely.
         Observe me now
         No monarch I vow,
            Was ever so afflicted!
LADY S.: I'm pleased with that poetical phrase,
         "A heavenly gaze,"
      But though you put it neatly,
         Say what you will,
         These paragraphs still
            Remain uncontradicted.

   Come, crush me this contemptible worm
         (*A forcible term*),
      If he's assailed you wrongly.
         The rage display,
         Which, as you say,
            Has moved your Majesty lately.
KING: Though I admit that forcible term
         "Contemptible worm,"
      Appeals to me most strongly,
         To treat this pest

As you suggest
    Would pain my Majesty greatly.
LADY S.: This writer lies!
KING: Yes, bother his eyes!
LADY S.: He lives, you say?
KING: In a sort of way.
LADY S.: Then have him shot.
KING: Decidedly not.
LADY S.: Or crush him flat.
KING: I cannot do that.
BOTH: O royal Rex,
    My/her blameless sex
    Abhors such conduct shady.
    You/I plead in vain,
    I/you will never gain
    Respectable English lady!
(*Dance of repudiation by Lady Sophy. Exit followed by King*)
March. Enter all the Court, heralding the arrival of the Princess Zara, who enters, escorted by Captain Fitzbattleaxe and four Troopers, all in the full uniform of the First Life Guards.

CHORUS.

Oh, maiden, rich
    In Girton lore
That wisdom which,
    We prized before,
We do confess
Is nothingness,
And rather less,
    Perhaps, than more.
On each of us
    Thy learning shed.
On calculus
    May we be fed.
And teach us, please,
To speak with ease,
All languages,
    Alive and dead!

Solo—Princess and Chorus.

Zara: Five years have flown since I took wing—
     Time flies, and his footstep ne'er retards—
  I'm the eldest daughter of your King.
Troop: And we are her escort—First Life Guards!
  On the royal yacht,
    When the waves were white,
  In a helmet hot
    And a tunic tight,
  And our great big boots,
    We defied the storm;
  For we're not recruits,
    And his uniform
  A well drilled trooper ne'er discards—
  And we are her escort—First Life Guards!
Zara: These gentlemen I present to you,
    The pride and boast of their barrack-yards;
  They've taken, O! such care of me!
Troop: For we are her escort—First Life Guards!
  When the tempest rose,
    And the ship went so—
  Do you suppose
    We were ill? No, no!
  Though a qualmish lot
    In a tunic tight,
  And a helmet hot,
    And a breastplate bright
  (*Which a well-drilled trooper ne'er discards*),
  We stood as her escort—First Life Guards!

Chorus.

  Knightsbridge nursemaids—serving fairies—
  Stars of proud Belgravian airies;
  At stern duty's call you leave them,
    Though you know how that must grieve them!
Zara: Tantantarara-rara-rara!
Fitz.: Trumpet-call of Princess Zara!

    ARTHUR SULLIVAN AND W.S. GILBERT

CHO.: That's trump-call, and they're all trump cards—
They are her escort—First Life Guards!

ENSEMBLE.

Chorus	Princess Zara and Fitzbattleaxe
Ladies	Oh! the hours are gold,
	And the joys untold,
Knightsbridge nursemaids,	When my eyes behold
etc.	My beloved Princess;
Men	And the years will seem
When the tempest rose, etc.	But a brief day-dream,
	In the joy extreme
	Of our happiness!

FULL CHORUS: Knightsbridge nursemaids, serving fairies, etc.

(*Enter King, Princess Nekaya and Kalyba, and Lady Sophy. As the King enters, the escort present arms*)

KING: Zara! my beloved daughter! Why, how well you look and how lovely you have grown! (*embraces her*)

ZARA: My dear father! (*embracing him*) And my two beautiful little sisters! (*embracing them*)

NEKAYA: Not beautiful.

KALYBA: Nice-looking.

ZARA: But first let me present to you the English warrior who commands my escort, and who has taken, O! such care of me during my voyage—Captain Fitzbattleaxe!

TROOPERS: The First Life Guards.
When the tempest rose,
And the ship went so—

(*Captain Fitzbattleaxe motions them to be silent. The Troopers place themselves in the four corners of the stage, standing at ease, immovably, as if on sentry. Each is surrounded by an admiring group of young ladies, of whom they take no notice*)

KING: (*to Capt. Fitz.*) Sir, you come from a country where every virtue flourishes. We trust that you will not criticize too severely such shortcomings as you may detect in our semi-barbarous society.

FITZ.: (*looking at Zara*) Sir, I have eyes for nothing but the blameless and the beautiful.

KING: We thank you—he is really very polite! (*Lady Sophy, who has been greatly scandalized by the attentions paid to the Lifeguardsmen by the young ladies, marches the Princesses Nekaya and Kalyba towards an exit*) Lady Sophy, do not leave us.

LADY S.: Sir, your children are young, and, so far, innocent. If they are to remain so, it is necessary that they be at once removed from the contamination of their present disgraceful surroundings. (*She marches them off*)

KING: (*whose attention has thus been called to the proceedings of the young ladies—aside*) Dear, dear! They really shouldn't. (*Aloud*) Captain Fitzbattleaxe—

FITZ.: Sir.

KING: Your Troopers appear to be receiving a troublesome amount of attention from those young ladies. I know how strict you English soldiers are, and I should be extremely distressed if anything occurred to shock their puritanical British sensitiveness.

FITZ.: Oh, I don't think there's any chance of that.

KING: You think not? They won't be offended?

FITZ.: Oh no! They are quite hardened to it. They get a good deal of that sort of thing, standing sentry at the Horse Guards.

KING: It's English, is it?

FITZ.: It's particularly English.

KING: Then, of course, it's all right. Pray proceed, ladies, it's particularly English. Come, my daughter, for we have much to say to each other.

ZARA: Farewell, Captain Fitzbattleaxe! I cannot thank you too emphatically for the devoted care with which you have watched over me during our long and eventful voyage.

DUET—Zara and Captain Fitzbattleaxe.

ZARA: Ah! gallant soldier, brave and true
    In tented field and tourney,
I grieve to have occasioned you
    So very long a journey.
A British warrior give up all—
    His home and island beauty—
When summoned to the trumpet call
    Of Regimental Duty!
CHO.: Tantantara-rara-rara!
    Trumpet call of the Princess Zara!

ENSEMBLE.

Men	Fitz. and Zara (*aside*)
A British warrior gives up all, etc.	Oh my joy, my pride,
	My delight to hide,
	Let us sing, aside,
Ladies	What in truth we feel,
	Let us whisper low
Knightsbridge nursemaids, etc.	Of our love's glad glow,
	Lest the truth we show
	We would fain conceal.

FITZ.: Such escort duty, as his due,
      To young Lifeguardsman falling
Completely reconciles him to
      His uneventful calling.
When soldier seeks Utopian glades
      In charge of Youth and Beauty,
Then pleasure merely masquerades
      As Regimental Duty!
ALL: Tantantarara-rara-rara!
      Trumpet-call of Princess Zara!

ENSEMBLE.

Men	Fitz. and Zara (*aside*)
A British warrior gives up all, etc.	Oh! my hours are gold,
	And the joys untold,
	When my eyes behold
Ladies	My beloved Princess;
	And the years will seem
Knightsbridge nursemaids, etc.	But a brief day-dream,
	In the job extreme
	Of our happiness!

(*Exeunt King and Zara in one direction, Lifeguardsmen and crowd in opposite direction. Enter, at back, Scaphio and Phantis, who watch Zara as she goes off. Scaphio is seated, shaking violently, and obviously under the influence of some strong emotion*)

PHANTIS: There—tell me, Scaphio, is she not beautiful? Can you wonder that I love her so passionately?

SCAPHIO: No. She is extraordinarily—miraculously lovely! Good heavens, what a singularly beautiful girl!

PHANTIS: I knew you would say so!

SCAPHIO: What exquisite charm of manner! What surprising delicacy of gesture! Why, she's a goddess! a very goddess!

PHANTIS: (*rather taken aback*) Yes—she's—she's an attractive girl.

SCAPHIO: Attractive? Why, you must be blind!—She's entrancing—enthralling—intoxicating! (*Aside*) God bless my heart, what's the matter with me?

PHANTIS: (*alarmed*) Yes. You—you promised to help me to get her father's consent, you know.

SCAPHIO: Promised! Yes, but the convulsion has come, my good boy! It is she—my ideal! Why, what's this? (*Staggering*) Phantis! Stop me—I'm going mad—mad with the love of her!

PHANTIS: Scaphio, compose yourself, I beg. The girl is perfectly opaque! Besides, remember—each of us is helpless without the other. You can't succeed without my consent, you know.

SCAPHIO: And you dare to threaten? Oh, ungrateful! When you came to me, palsied with love for this girl, and implored my assistance, did I not unhesitatingly promise it? And this is the return you make? Out of my sight, ingrate! (*Aside*) Dear! dear! what is the matter with me? (*Enter Capt. Fitzbattleaxe and Zara*)

ZARA: Dear me. I'm afraid we are interrupting a tete-a-tete.

SCAPHIO: (*breathlessly*) No, no. You come very appropriately. To be brief, we—we love you—this man and I—madly—passionately!

ZARA: Sir!

SCAPHIO: And we don't know how we are to settle which of us is to marry you.

FITZ.: Zara, this is very awkward.

SCAPHIO: (*very much overcome*) I—I am paralyzed by the singular radiance of your extraordinary loveliness. I know I am incoherent. I never was like this before—it shall not occur again. I—shall be fluent, presently.

ZARA: (*aside*) Oh, dear, Captain Fitzbattleaxe, what is to be done?

FITZ.: (*aside*) Leave it to me—I'll manage it. (*Aloud*) It's a common situation. Why not settle it in the English fashion?

BOTH: The English fashion? What is that?

FITZ.: It's very simple. In England, when two gentlemen are in love with the same lady, and until it is settled which gentleman is to blow out the brains of the other, it is provided, by the Rival Admirers' Clauses Consolidation Act, that the lady shall be entrusted to an officer of Household Cavalry as stakeholder, who is bound to hand her over to the survivor (*on the Tontine principle*) in a good condition of substantial and decorative repair.

SCAPHIO: Reasonable wear and tear and damages by fire excepted?

FITZ.: Exactly.

PHANTIS: Well, that seems very reasonable. (*To Scaphio*) What do you say—Shall we entrust her to this officer of Household Cavalry? It will give us time.

SCAPHIO: (*trembling violently*) I—I am not at present in a condition to think it out coolly—but if he is an officer of Household Cavalry, and if the Princess consents—

ZARA: Alas, dear sirs, I have no alternative—under the Rival Admirers' Clauses Consolidation Act!

FITZ.: Good—then that's settled.

QUARTET.

Fitzbattleaxe, Zara, Scaphio, and Phantis.

FITZ.: It's understood, I think, all round
That, by the English custom bound
I hold the lady safe and sound
    In trust for either rival,
Until you clearly testify
By sword and pistol, by and by,
Which gentleman prefers to die,
    And which prefers survival.

ENSEMBLE.

Sca. and Phan.	Zara and Fitz
Its clearly understood all round	We stand, I think, on safish ground
That, by your English custom bound	Our senses weak it will astound
He holds the lady safe and sound	If either gentleman is found
In trust for either rival,	Prepared to meet his rival.
Until we clearly testify	Their machinations we defy;

By sword or pistol, by and by

Which gentleman prefers to die,

    Which prefers survival.

We won't be parted, you
    and I—

Of bloodshed each is rather
    shy—

They both prefer survival

PHAN.: If I should die and he should live
(*aside to Fitz.*) To you, without reserve, I give
    Her heart so young and sensitive,
    And all her predilections.
SCA.: If he should live and I should die,
(*aside to Fitz.*) I see no kind of reason why
    You should not, if you wish it, try
    To gain her young affections.

ENSEMBLE.

Sca. and Phant.	Fitz and Zara
If I should die and you should live	As both of us are positive
To this young officer I give	That both of them intend to live,
Her heart so soft and sensitive,	There's nothing in the case to give
And all her predilections.	Us cause for grave reflections.
If you should live and I should die	As both will live and neither die
I see no kind of reason why	I see no kind of reason why
He should not, if he chooses, try To win her young affections.	I should not, if I wish it, try To gain your young affections!

(*Exit Scaphio and Phantis together*)

DUET—Zara and Fitzbattleaxe.

ENSEMBLE: Oh admirable art!
    Oh, neatly-planned intention!
    Oh, happy intervention—
      Oh, well constructed plot!

ARTHUR SULLIVAN AND W.S. GILBERT

When sages try to part
    Two loving hearts in fusion,
    Their wisdom's delusion,
        And learning serves them not!
FITZ.: Until quit plain
        Is their intent,
    These sages twain
        I represent.
    Now please infer
        That, nothing loth,
    You're henceforth, as it were,
        Engaged to marry both—
    Then take it that I represent the two—
    On that hypothesis, what would you do?
ZARA (*aside*): What would I do? what would I do?
(*To Fitz.*) In such a case,
        Upon your breast,
    My blushing face
        I think I'd rest—(*doing so*)
    Then perhaps I might
        Demurely say—
    "I find this breastplate bright
        Is sorely in the way!"
FITZ.: Our mortal race
        Is never blest—
    There's no such case
        As perfect rest;
    Some petty blight
        Asserts its sway—
    Some crumbled roseleaf light
        Is always in the way!
(*Exit Fitzbattleaxe. Manet Zara*)
(*Enter King*)
KING: My daughter! At last we are alone together.
ZARA: Yes, and I'm glad we are, for I want to speak to you very
    seriously. Do you know this paper?
KING: (*aside*) Da—! (*Aloud*) Oh yes—I've—I've seen it. Where in the
    world did you get this from?
ZARA: It was given to me by Lady Sophy—my sisters' governess.

KING: (*aside*) Lady Sophy's an angel, but I do sometimes wish she'd mind her own business! (*Aloud*) It's—ha! ha!—it's rather humorous.

ZARA: I see nothing humorous in it. I only see that you, the despotic King of this country, are made the subject of the most scandalous insinuations. Why do you permit these things?

KING: Well, they appeal to my sense of humor. It's the only really comic paper in Utopia, and I wouldn't be without it for the world.

ZARA: If it had any literary merit I could understand it.

KING: Oh, it has literary merit. Oh, distinctly, it has literary merit.

ZARA: My dear father, it's mere ungrammatical twaddle.

KING: Oh, it's not ungrammatical. I can't allow that. Unpleasantly personal, perhaps, but written with an epigrammatical point that is very rare nowadays—very rare indeed.

ZARA: (*looking at cartoon*) Why do they represent you with such a big nose?

KING: (*looking at cartoon*) Eh? Yes, it is a big one! Why, the fact is that, in the cartoons of a comic paper, the size of your nose always varies inversely as the square of your popularity. It's the rule.

ZARA: Then you must be at a tremendous discount just now! I see a notice of a new piece called "King Tuppence," in which an English tenor has the audacity to personate you on a public stage. I can only say that I am surprised that any English tenor should lend himself to such degrading personalities.

KING: Oh, he's not really English. As it happens he's a Utopian, but he calls himself English.

ZARA: Calls himself English?

KING: Yes. Bless you, they wouldn't listen to any tenor who didn't call himself English.

ZARA: And you permit this insolent buffoon to caricature you in a pointless burlesque! My dear father—if you were a free agent, you would never permit these outrages.

KING: (*almost in tears*) Zara—I—I admit I am not altogether a free agent. I—I am controlled. I try to make the best of it, but sometimes I find it very difficult—very difficult indeed. Nominally a Despot, I am, between ourselves, the helpless tool of two unscrupulous Wise Men, who insist on my falling in with all their wishes and threaten to denounce me for immediate explosion if I remonstrate! (*Breaks down completely*)

ARTHUR SULLIVAN AND W.S. GILBERT

ZARA: My poor father! Now listen to me. With a view to remodelling the political and social institutions of Utopia, I have brought with me six Representatives of the principal causes that have tended to make England the powerful, happy, and blameless country which the consensus of European civilization has declared it to be. Place yourself unreservedly in the hands of these gentlemen, and they will reorganize your country on a footing that will enable you to defy your persecutors. They are all now washing their hands after their journey. Shall I introduce them?

KING: My dear Zara, how can I thank you? I will consent to anything that will release me from the abominable tyranny of these two men. (*Calling*) What ho! Without there! (*Enter Calynx*) Summon my Court without an instant's delay! (*Exit Calynx*)

FINALE.

Enter every one, except the Flowers of Progress.

CHORUS.

Although your Royal summons to appear
From courtesy was singularly free,
Obedient to that summons we are here—
What would your Majesty?

RECITATIVE—King.

My worthy people, my beloved daughter
Most thoughtfully has brought with her from England
The types of all the causes that have made
That great and glorious country what it is.

CHORUS: Oh, joy unbounded!

SCA., TAR., PHAN.: (*aside*) Why, what does this mean?

RECITATIVE—Zara.

Attend to me, Utopian populace,
Ye South Pacific island viviparians;
All, in the abstract, types of courtly grace,

Yet, when compared with Britain's glorious race,
But little better than half clothed Barbarians!

CHORUS.

Yes! Contrasted when
With Englishmen,
Are little better than half-clothed barbarians!
Enter all the Flowers of Progress, led by Fitzbattleaxe.

SOLOS—Zara and the Flowers of Progress.

(*Presenting Captain Fitzbattleaxe*)
When Britain sounds the trump of war
(*And Europe trembles*),
The army of the conqueror
In serried ranks assemble;
'Tis then this warrior's eyes and sabre gleam
For our protection—
He represents a military scheme
In all its proud perfection!
CHORUS: Yes—yes
He represents a military scheme
In all its proud perfection.
Ulahlica! Ulahlica! Ulahlica!

SOLO—Zara.

(*Presenting Sir Bailey Barre, Q.C., M.P.*)
A complicated gentleman allow to present,
Of all the arts and faculties the terse embodiment,
He's a great arithmetician who can demonstrate with ease
That two and two are three or five or anything you please;
An eminent Logician who can make it clear to you
That black is white—when looked at from the proper point of
view;
A marvelous Philologist who'll undertake to show
That "yes" is but another and a neater form of "no."
SIR BAILEY: Yes—yes—yes—

"Yes" is but another and a neater form of "no."
All preconceived ideas on any subject I can scout,
And demonstrate beyond all possibility of doubt,
That whether you're an honest man or whether you're a thief
Depends on whose solicitor has given me my brief.

CHORUS: Yes—yes—yes
   That whether your'e an honest man, etc.
    Ulahlica! Ulahlica! Ulahlica!

ZARA: (*Presenting Lord Dramaleigh and County Councillor*)
   What these may be, Utopians all,
    Perhaps you'll hardly guess—
They're types of England's physical
  And moral cleanliness.
This is a Lord High Chamberlain,
  Of purity the gauge—
He'll cleanse our court from moral stain
  And purify our Stage.

LORD D.: Yes—yes—yes
Court reputations I revise,
And presentations scrutinize,
New plays I read with jealous eyes,
  And purify the Stage.

CHORUS: Court reputations, etc.

ZARA: This County Councillor acclaim,
   Great Britain's latest toy—
On anything you like to name
   His talents he'll employ—

All streets and squares he'll purify
  Within your city walls,
And keep meanwhile a modest eye
  On wicked music halls.

C.C.: Yes—yes—yes
In towns I make improvements great,
Which go to swell the County Rate—
I dwelling-houses sanitate,
  And purify the Halls!

CHORUS: In towns he makes improvements great, etc.
   Ulahlica! Ulahlica! Ulahlica!

Solo—Zara.

(*Presenting Mr. Goldbury*)

A Company Promoter this with special education,
Which teaches what Contango means and also Backwardation—
To speculators he supplies a grand financial leaven,
Time was when two were company—but now it must be seven.

Mr. Gold.: Yes—yes—yes
Stupendous loans to foreign thrones
    I've largely advocated;
In ginger-pops and peppermint-drops
    I've freely speculated;
Then mines of gold, of wealth untold,
    Successfully I've floated
And sudden falls in apple-stalls
    Occasionally quoted.
And soon or late I always call
    For Stock Exchange quotation—
No schemes too great and none too small
    For Companification!

Chorus: Yes! Yes! Yes! No schemes too great, etc.
    Ulahlica! Ulahlica! Ulahlica!

Zara: (*Presenting Capt. Sir Edward Corcoran, R.N.*)
And lastly I present
    Great Britain's proudest boast,
Who from the blows
Of foreign foes
    Protects her sea-girt coast—
And if you ask him in respectful tone,
He'll show you how you may protect your own!

Solo—Captain Corcoran.

I'm Captain Corcoran, K.C.B.,
I'll teach you how we rule the sea,
    And terrify the simple Gauls;
And how the Saxon and the Celt
Their Europe-shaking blows have dealt
With Maxim gun and Nordenfelt

(*Or will when the occasion calls*).
If sailor-like you'd play your cards,
Unbend your sails and lower your yards,
    Unstep your masts—you'll never want 'em more.
Though we're no longer hearts of oak,
Yet we can steer and we can stoke,
And thanks to coal, and thanks to coke,
    We never run a ship ashore!
ALL: What never?
CAPT.: No, never!
ALL: What never?
CAPT.: Hardly ever!
ALL: Hardly ever run a ship ashore!
    Then give three cheers, and three cheers more,
    For the tar who never runs his ship ashore;
    Then give three cheers, and three cheers more,
        For he never runs his ship ashore!

CHORUS.

All hail, ye types of England's power—
    Ye heaven-enlightened band!
We bless the day and bless the hour
    That brought you to our land.

QUARTET.

Ye wanderers from a mighty State,
Oh, teach us how to legislate—
Your lightest word will carry weight,
    In our attentive ears.
Oh, teach the natives of this land
(*Who are not quick to understand*)
How to work off their social and
    Political arrears!
CAPT. FITZ.: Increase your army!
LORD D.: Purify your court!
CAPT. CORC.: Get up your steam and cut your canvas short!
SIR B.: To speak on both sides teach your sluggish brains!
MR. B.: Widen your thoroughfares, and flush your drains!

Mr. Gold.: Utopia's much too big for one small head—
I'll float it as a Company Limited!
King: A Company Limited? What may that be?
    The term, I rather think, is new to me.
Chorus: A company limited? etc.
    Sca, Phant, and Tara (*Aside*)
        What does he mean? What does he mean?
            Give us a kind of clue!
        What does he mean? What does he mean?
            What is he going to do?

Song—Mr. Goldbury.

Some seven men form an Association
    (*If possible, all Peers and Baronets*),
The start off with a public declaration
    To what extent they mean to pay their debts.
That's called their Capital; if they are wary
    They will not quote it at a sum immense.
The figure's immaterial—it may vary
    From eighteen million down to eighteenpence.
        I should put it rather low;
        The good sense of doing so
    Will be evident at once to any debtor.
        When it's left to you to say
        What amount you mean to pay,
    Why, the lower you can put it at, the better.
Chorus: When it's left to you to say, etc.
    They then proceed to trade with all who'll trust 'em
        Quite irrespective of their capital
    (*It's shady, but it's sanctified by custom*);
        Bank, Railway, Loan, or Panama Canal.
    You can't embark on trading too tremendous—
        It's strictly fair, and based on common sense—
    If you succeed, your profits are stupendous—
        And if you fail, pop goes your eighteenpence.

    Make the money-spinner spin!
    For you only stand to win,

And you'll never with dishonesty be twitted.
    For nobody can know,
    To a million or so,
To what extent your capital's committed!
CHORUS: No, nobody can know, etc.

If you come to grief, and creditors are craving
    (For nothing that is planned by mortal head
Is certain in this Vale of Sorrow—saving
    That one's Liability is Limited),—
Do you suppose that signifies perdition?
    If so, you're but a monetary dunce—
You merely file a Winding-Up Petition,
    And start another Company at once!
    Though a Rothschild you may be
    In your own capacity,
As a Company you've come to utter sorrow—
    But the Liquidators say,
    "Never mind—you needn't pay,"
So you start another company to-morrow!
CHORUS: But the liquidators say, etc.
KING: Well, at first sight it strikes us as dishonest,
    But if it's good enough for virtuous England—
    The first commercial country in the world—
    It's good enough for us.
    Sca., Phan., Tar. (*aside to the King*)
                You'd best take care—
    Please recollect we have not been consulted.
KING: And do I understand that Great Britain
    Upon this Joint Stock principle is governed?
MR. G.: We haven't come to that, exactly—but
    We're tending rapidly in that direction.
    The date's not distant.
KING: (*enthusiastically*) We will be before you!
    We'll go down in posterity renowned
    As the First Sovereign in Christendom
    Who registered his Crown and Country under
    The Joint Stock Company's Act of Sixty-Two.
ALL: Ulahlica!

Henceforward, of a verity,
    With Fame ourselves we link—
We'll go down to Posterity
    Of sovereigns all the pink!

Sca., Phan., Tar.: (*aside to King*)

If you've the mad temerity
    Our wishes thus to blink,
You'll go down to Posterity,
    Much earlier than you think!

Tar.: (*correcting them*)

    He'll go up to Posterity,
        If I inflict the blow!

Sca., Phan.: (*angrily*)

    He'll go down to Posterity—
        We think we ought to know!

Tar.: (*explaining*) He'll go up to Posterity,
    Blown up with dynamite!

Sca., Phan.: (*apologetically*)

    He'll go up to Posterity,
        Of course he will, you're right!

Ensemble.

King, Lady Sophy, Nek., Kal., Calynx and Chorus	Sca., Phan., and Tar. (*aside*)	Fitz. and Zara (*aside*)
Henceforward of a verity,	If he has the temerity	Who love with all sincerity;
With fame ourselves we link—	Our wishes thus to blink	Their lives may safely link.
And go down to Posterity,	He'll go up to Posterity	And as for our posterity
Of sovereigns all pink!	Much earlier than they think!	We don't care what they think!

Chorus.

Let's seal this mercantile pact—
 The step we ne'er shall rue—
It gives whatever we lacked—
 The statement's strictly true.
All hail, astonishing Fact!
 All hail, Invention new—
The Joint Stock Company's Act—
 The Act of Sixty-Two!

END OF ACT I

Act II

Recitative—Fitzbattleaxe.

Oh, Zara, my beloved one, bear with me!
Ah, do not laugh at my attempted C!
Repent not, mocking maid, thy girlhood's choice—
The fervour of my love affects my voice!

Song—Fitzbattleaxe.

A tenor, all singers above
   (*This doesn't admit of a question*),
      Should keep himself quiet,
      Attend to his diet
   And carefully nurse his digestion;
But when he is madly in love
   It's certain to tell on his singing—
      You can't do the proper chromatics
      With proper emphatics
   When anguish your bosom is wringing!
When distracted with worries in plenty,
And his pulse is a hundred and twenty,
And his fluttering bosom the slave of mistrust is,
A tenor can't do himself justice,
   Now observe—(*sings a high note*),
You see, I can't do myself justice!
I could sing if my fervour were mock,
   It's easy enough if you're acting—
      But when one's emotion
      Is born of devotion
   You mustn't be over-exacting.
One ought to be firm as a rock
   To venture a shake in vibrato,
      When fervour's expected

Keep cool and collected
Or never attempt agitato.
But, of course, when his tongue is of leather,
And his lips appear pasted together,
And his sensitive palate as dry as a crust is,
A tenor can't do himself justice.
Now observe—(*sings a high note*),
It's no use—I can't do myself justice!

ZARA: Why, Arthur, what does it matter? When the higher qualities of the heart are all that can be desired, the higher notes of the voice are matters of comparative insignificance. Who thinks slightingly of the cocoanut because it is husky? Besides (*demurely*), you are not singing for an engagement (*putting her hand in his*), you have that already!

FITZ.: How good and wise you are! How unerringly your practiced brain winnows the wheat from the chaff—the material from the merely incidental!

ZARA: My Girton training, Arthur. At Girton all is wheat, and idle chaff is never heard within its walls! But tell me, is not all working marvelously well? Have not our Flowers of Progress more than justified their name?

FITZ.: We have indeed done our best. Captain Corcoran and I have, in concert, thoroughly remodeled the sister-services—and upon so sound a basis that the South Pacific trembles at the name of Utopia!

ZARA: How clever of you!

FITZ.: Clever? Not a bit. It's easy as possible when the Admiralty and Horse Guards are not there to interfere. And so with the others. Freed from the trammels imposed upon them by idle Acts of Parliament, all have given their natural talents full play and introduced reforms which, even in England, were never dreamt of!

ZARA: But perhaps the most beneficent changes of all has been effected by Mr. Goldbury, who, discarding the exploded theory that some strange magic lies hidden in the number Seven, has applied the Limited Liability principle to individuals, and every man, woman, and child is now a Company Limited with liability restricted to the amount of his declared Capital! There is not a christened baby in Utopia who has not already issued his little Prospectus!

FITZ.: Marvelous is the power of a Civilization which can transmute, by a word, a Limited Income into an Income Limited.

ZARA: Reform has not stopped here—it has been applied even to the costume of our people. Discarding their own barbaric dress, the natives of our land have unanimously adopted the tasteful fashions of England in all their rich entirety. Scaphio and Phantis have undertaken a contract to supply the whole of Utopia with clothing designed upon the most approved English models—and the first Drawing-Room under the new state of things is to be held here this evening.

FITZ.: But Drawing-Rooms are always held in the afternoon.

ZARA: Ah, we've improved upon that. We all look so much better by candlelight! And when I tell you, dearest, that my Court train has just arrived, you will understand that I am longing to go and try it on.

FITZ.: Then we must part?

ZARA: Necessarily, for a time.

FITZ.: Just as I wanted to tell you, with all the passionate enthusiasm of my nature, how deeply, how devotedly I love you!

ZARA: Hush! Are these the accents of a heart that really feels? True love does not indulge in declamation—its voice is sweet, and soft, and low. The west wind whispers when he woos the poplars!

DUET—Zara and Fitzbattleaxe.

ZARA: Words of love too loudly spoken
    Ring their own untimely knell;
Noisy vows are rudely broken,
    Soft the song of Philomel.
Whisper sweetly, whisper slowly,
    Hour by hour and day by day;
Sweet and low as accents holy
    Are the notes of lover's lay.

BOTH: Sweet and low, etc.

FITZ.: Let the conqueror, flushed with glory,
    Bid his noisy clarions bray;
Lovers tell their artless story
    In a whispered virelay.
False is he whose vows alluring
    Make the listening echoes ring;

Sweet and low when all-enduring
   Are the songs that lovers sing!

BOTH: Sweet and low, etc.

(*Exit Zara. Enter King dressed as Field-Marshal*)

KING: To a Monarch who has been accustomed to the uncontrolled use of his limbs, the costume of a British Field-Marshal is, perhaps, at first, a little cramping. Are you sure that this is all right? It's not a practical joke, is it? No one has a keener sense of humor than I have, but the First Statutory Cabinet Council of Utopia Limited must be conducted with dignity and impressiveness. Now, where are the other five who signed the Articles of Association?

FITZ.: Sir, they are here.

(*Enter Lord Dramaleigh, Captain Corcoran, Sir Bailey Barre, Mr. Blushington, and Mr. Goldbury from different entrances*)

KING: Oh! (*Addressing them*) Gentlemen, our daughter holds her first Drawing-Room in half an hour, and we shall have time to make our half-yearly report in the interval. I am necessarily unfamiliar with the forms of an English Cabinet Council—perhaps the Lord Chamberlain will kindly put us in the way of doing the thing properly, and with due regard to the solemnity of the occasion.

LORD D.: Certainly—nothing simpler. Kindly bring your chairs forward—His Majesty will, of course, preside.

(*They range their chairs across stage like Christy Minstrels. King sits center, Lord Dramaleigh on his left, Mr. Goldbury on his right, Captain Corcoran left of Lord Dramaleigh, Captain Fitzbattleaxe right of Mr. Goldbury, Mr. Blushington extreme right, Sir Bailey Barre extreme left*)

KING: Like this?

LORD D.: Like this.

KING: We take your word for it that this is all right. You are not making fun of us? This is in accordance with the practice at the Court of St. James's?

LORD D.: Well, it is in accordance with the practice at the Court of St. James's Hall.

KING: Oh! it seems odd, but never mind.

SONG—King.

Society has quite forsaken all her wicked courses.
Which empties our police courts, and abolishes divorces.

CHORUS: Divorce is nearly obsolete in England.

KING: No tolerance we show to undeserving rank and splendour; For the higher his position is, the greater the offender.

CHORUS: That's maxim that is prevalent in England.

KING: No peeress at our drawing-room before the Presence passes
Who wouldn't be accepted by the lower middle-classes. Each shady dame, whatever be her rank, is bowed out neatly.

CHORUS: In short, this happy country has been Anglicized completely
Is really is surprising
What a thorough Anglicizing
We have brought about—Utopia's quite another land;
In her enterprising movements,
She is England—with improvements,
Which we dutifully offer to our mother-land!

KING: Our city we have beautified—we've done it willy-nilly—And all that isn't Belgrave Square is Strand and Piccadilly.

CHORUS: We haven't any slummeries in England!

KING: The chamberlain our native stage has purged beyond a question.
Of "risky" situation and indelicate suggestion;
No piece is tolerated if it's costumed indiscreetly—

CHORUS: In short this happy country has been Anglicized completely!
It really is surprising, etc.

KING: Our peerage we've remodelled on an intellectual basis, which certainly is rough on our hereditary races—

CHORUS: We are going to remodel it in England.

KING: The Brewers and the Cotton Lords no longer seek admission, and literary merit meets with proper recognition—

CHORUS: As literary merit does in England!

KING: Who knows but we may count among our intellectual chickens
Like you, an Earl of Thackery and p'r'aps a Duke of Dickens—
Lord Fildes and Viscount Millais (*when they come*) we'll welcome sweetly—

CHORUS: In short, this happy country has been Anglicized completely!
It really is surprising, etc.

(*At the end all rise and replace their chairs*)

KING: Now, then for our first Drawing-Room. Where are the Princesses? What an extraordinary thing it is that since European looking-glasses have been supplied to the Royal bedrooms my daughters are invariably late!

LORD D.: Sir, their Royal Highnesses await your pleasure in the Ante-room.

KING: Oh. Then request them to do us the favor to enter at once.

(*Enter all the Royal Household, including (besides the Lord Chamberlain) the Vice-Chamberlain, the Master of the Horse, the Master of the Buckhounds, the Lord High Treasurer, the Lord Steward, the Comptroller of the Household, the Lord-in-Waiting, the Field Officer in Brigade Waiting, the Gold and Silver Stick, and the Gentlemen Ushers. Then enter the three Princesses (their trains carried by Pages of Honor), Lady Sophy, and the Ladies-in-Waiting*)

KING: My daughters, we are about to attempt a very solemn ceremonial, so no giggling, if you please. Now, my Lord Chamberlain, we are ready.

LORD D.: Then, ladies and gentlemen, places, if you please. His Majesty will take his place in front of the throne, and will be so obliging as to embrace all the debutantes. (LADY SOPHY *much shocked*)

KING: What—must I really?

LORD D.: Absolutely indispensable.

KING: More jam for the Palace Peeper!

(*The King takes his place in front of the throne, the Princess Zara on his left, the two younger Princesses on the left of Zara.*)

KING: Now, is every one in his place?

LORD D.: Every one is in his place.

KING: Then let the revels commence.

(*Enter the ladies attending the Drawing-Room. They give their cards to the Groom-in-Waiting, who passes them to the Lord-in-Waiting, who passes them to the Vice-Chamberlain, who passes them to the Lord Chamberlain, who reads the names to the King as each lady approaches. The ladies curtsey in succession to the King and the three Princesses, and pass out. When all the presentations have been accomplished, the King, Princesses, and Lady Sophy come forward, and all the ladies re-enter*)

RECITATIVE—King.

This ceremonial our wish displays
To copy all Great Britain's courtly ways.
Though lofty aims catastrophe entail,
We'll gloriously succeed or nobly fail!

Unaccompanied Chorus.

Eagle High in Cloudland soaring—
    Sparrow twittering on a reed—
Tiger in the jungle roaring—
    Frightened fawn in grassy mead—
Let the eagle, not the sparrow,
Be the object of your arrow—
    Fix the tiger with your eye—
    Pass the fawn in pity by.
    Glory then will crown the day—
    Glory, glory, anyway!

Exit all.
Enter Scaphio and Phantis, now dressed as judges in red and ermine robes and undress wigs. They come down stage melodramatically—working together.

Duet—Scaphio and Phantis.

SCA.: With fury deep we burn
PHAN.: We do—
SCA.: We fume with smothered rage—
PHAN.: We do—
SCA.: These Englishmen who rule supreme,
    Their undertaking they redeem
    By stifling every harmless scheme
        In which we both engage—
Phan.: They do—
SCA.: In which we both engage—
PHAN.: We think it is our turn—
SCA.: We do—
PHAN.: We think our turn has come—
SCA.: We do.
PHAN.: These Englishmen, they must prepare
    To seek at once their native air.
    The King as heretofore, we swear,
    Shall be beneath our thumb—
SCA.: He shall—
PHAN.: Shall be beneath out thumb—
SCA.: He shall.

BOTH: (*with great energy*)
>For this mustn't be, and this won't do.
>If you'll back me, then I'll back you,
>>No, this won't do,
>>No, this mustn't be.
>With fury deep we burn. . .

Enter the King.

KING: Gentlemen, gentlemen—really! This unseemly display of energy within the Royal precincts is altogether unpardonable. Pray, what do you complain of?

SCAPHIO: (*furiously*) What do we complain of? Why, through the innovations introduced by the Flowers of Progress all our harmless schemes for making a provision for our old age are ruined. Our Matrimonial Agency is at a standstill, our Cheap Sherry business is in bankruptcy, our Army Clothing contracts are paralyzed, and even our Society paper, the Palace Peeper, is practically defunct!

KING: Defunct? Is that so? Dear, dear, I am truly sorry.

SCAPHIO: Are you aware that Sir Bailey Barre has introduced a law of libel by which all editors of scurrilous newspapers are publicly flogged—as in England? And six of our editors have resigned in succession! Now, the editor of a scurrilous paper can stand a good deal—he takes a private thrashing as a matter of course—it's considered in his salary—but no gentleman likes to be publicly flogged.

KING: Naturally. I shouldn't like it myself.

PHANTIS: Then our Burlesque Theater is absolutely ruined!

KING: Dear me. Well, theatrical property is not what it was.

PHANTIS: Are you aware that the Lord Chamberlain, who has his own views as to the best means of elevating the national drama, has declined to license any play that is not in blank verse and three hundred years old—as in England?

SCAPHIO: And as if that wasn't enough, the County Councillor has ordered a four-foot wall to be built up right across the proscenium, in case of fire—as in England.

PHANTIS: It's so hard on the company—who are liable to be roasted alive—and this has to be met by enormously increased salaries—as in England.

SCAPHIO: You probably know that we've contracted to supply the entire nation with a complete English outfit. But perhaps you do not know that, when we send in our bills, our customers plead liability limited to a declared capital of eighteenpence, and apply to be dealt with under the Winding-up Act—as in England?

KING: Really, gentlemen, this is very irregular. If you will be so good as to formulate a detailed list of your grievances in writing, addressed to the Secretary of Utopia Limited, they will be laid before the Board, in due course, at their next monthly meeting.

SCAPHIO: Are we to understand that we are defied?

KING: That is the idea I intended to convey.

PHANTIS: Defied! We are defied!

SCAPHIO: (*furiously*) Take care—you know our powers. Trifle with us, and you die!

TRIO—Scaphio, Phantis, and King.

SCA.: If you think that, when banded in unity,
We may both be defied with impunity,
You are sadly misled of a verity!

PHAN.: If you value repose and tranquility,
You'll revert to a state of docility,
Or prepare to regret your temerity!

KING: If my speech is unduly refractory
You will find it a course satisfactory
At an early Board meeting to show it up.
Though if proper excuse you can trump any,
You may wind up a Limited Company,
You cannot conveniently blow it up!

(*Scaphio and Phantis thoroughly baffled*)

KING: (*Dancing quietly*)
Whene'er I chance to baffle you
I, also, dance a step or two—
Of this now guess the hidden sense:

(*Scaphio and Phantis consider the question as King continues dancing quietly—then give it up*)

It means complete indifference!

SCA. AND PHAN.: Of course it does—indifference!
It means complete indifference!

(*King dancing quietly. Sca. and Phan. dancing furiously*)

SCA. AND PHAN.: As we've a dance for every mood

With pas de trois we will conclude,
What this may mean you all may guess—
It typifies remorselessness!

KING: It means unruffled cheerfulness!

(*King dances off placidly as Scaphio and Phantis dance furiously*)

PHANTIS: (*breathless*) He's right—we are helpless! He's no longer a
human being—he's a Corporation, and so long as he confines
himself to his Articles of Association we can't touch him! What
are we to do?

SCAPHIO: Do? Raise a Revolution, repeal the Act of Sixty-Two, reconvert
him into an individual, and insist on his immediate explosion! (*Tarara
enters*) Tarara, come here; you're the very man we want.

TARARA: Certainly, allow me. (*Offers a cracker to each; they snatch them
away impatiently*) That's rude.

SCAPHIO: We have no time for idle forms. You wish to succeed to the
throne?

TARARA: Naturally.

SCAPHIO: Then you won't unless you join us. The King has defied us,
and, as matters stand, we are helpless. So are you. We must devise
some plot at once to bring the people about his ears.

TARARA: A plot?

PHANTIS: Yes, a plot of superhuman subtlety. Have you such a thing
about you?

TARARA: (*feeling*) No, I think not. No. There's one on my dressing-table.

SCAPHIO: We can't wait—we must concoct one at once, and put it into
execution without delay. There is not a moment to spare!

TRIO—Scaphio, Phantis, and Tarara.

Ensemble.

With wily brain upon the spot
    A private plot we'll plan,
The most ingenious private plot
    Since private plots began.
That's understood. So far we've got
And, striking while the iron's hot,
We'll now determine like a shot
The details of this private plot.

Sca.: I think we ought—(*whispers*)

Phan. and Tar.: Such bosh I never heard!

Phan.: Ah! happy thought!—(*whispers*)

Sca. and Tar.: How utterly dashed absurd!

Tar.: I'll tell you how—(*whispers*)

Sca and Phan.: Why, what put that in your head?

Sca.: I've got it now—(*whispers*)

Phan. and Tar.: Oh, take him away to bed!

Phan.: Oh, put him to bed!

Tar.: Oh, put him to bed!

Sca.: What, put me to bed?

Phan. and Tar.: Yes, certainly put him to bed!

Sca.: But, bless me, don't you see—

Phan.: Do listen to me, I pray—

Tar.: It certainly seems to me—

Sca.: Bah—this is the only way!

Phan.: It's rubbish absurd you growl!

Tar.: You talk ridiculous stuff!

Sca.: You're a drivelling barndoor owl!

Phan.: You're a vapid and vain old muff!

(*All, coming down to audience*)

So far we haven't quite solved the plot—
They're not a very ingenious lot—
    But don't be unhappy,
    It's still on the tapis,
We'll presently hit on a capital plot!

Sca.: Suppose we all—(*whispers*)

Phan.: Now there I think you're right.
    Then we might all—(*whispers*)

Tar.: That's true, we certainly might.
    I'll tell you what—(*whispers*)

Sca.: We will if we possibly can.
    Then on the spot—(*whispers*)

Phan. and Tar.: Bravo! A capital plan!

Sca.: That's exceedingly neat and new!

Phan.: Exceedingly new and neat.

Tar.: I fancy that that will do.

Sca.: It's certainly very complete.

Phan.: Well done you sly old sap!

TAR.: Bravo, you cunning old mole!

SCA.: You very ingenious chap!

PHAN.: You intellectual soul!

(*All, coming down and addressing audience*)

At last a capital plan we've got

We won't say how and we won't say what:

It's safe in my noddle—

Now off we will toddle,

And slyly develop this capital plot!

(*Business. Exeunt Scaphio and Phantis in one direction, and Tarara in the other*)

(*Enter Lord Dramaleigh and Mr. Goldbury*)

LORD D.: Well, what do you think of our first South Pacific Drawing-Room? Allowing for a slight difficulty with the trains, and a little want of familiarity with the use of the rouge-pot, it was, on the whole, a meritorious affair?

GOLD.: My dear Dramaleigh, it redounds infinitely to your credit.

LORD D.: One or two judicious innovations, I think?

GOLD.: Admirable. The cup of tea and the plate of mixed biscuits were a cheap and effective inspiration.

LORD D.: Yes—my idea entirely. Never been done before.

GOLD.: Pretty little maids, the King's youngest daughters, but timid.

LORD D.: That'll wear off. Young.

GOLD.: That'll wear off. Ha! here they come, by George! And without the Dragon! What can they have done with her?

(*Enter Nekaya and Kalyba timidly*)

NEKAYA: Oh, if you please, Lady Sophy has sent us in here, because Zara and Captain Fitzbattleaxe are going on, in the garden, in a manner which no well-conducted young ladies ought to witness.

LORD D.: Indeed, we are very much obliged to her Ladyship.

KALYBA: Are you? I wonder why.

NEKAYA: Don't tell us if it's rude.

LORD D.: Rude? Not at all. We are obliged to Lady Sophy because she has afforded us the pleasure of seeing you.

NEKAYA: I don't think you ought to talk to us like that.

KALYBA: It's calculated to turn our heads.

NEKAYA: Attractive girls cannot be too particular.

KALYBA: Oh pray, pray do not take advantage of our unprotected innocence.

GOLD.: Pray be reassured—you are in no danger whatever.

LORD D.: But may I ask—is this extreme delicacy—this shrinking sensitiveness—a general characteristic of Utopian young ladies?

NEKAYA: Oh no; we are crack specimens.

KALYBA: We are the pick of the basket. Would you mind not coming quite so near? Thank you.

NEKAYA: And please don't look at us like that; it unsettles us.

KALYBA: And we don't like it. At least, we do like it; but it's wrong.

NEKAYA: We have enjoyed the inestimable privilege of being educated by a most refined and easily shocked English lady, on the very strictest English principles.

GOLD.: But, my dear young ladies—

KALYBA: Oh, don't! You mustn't. It's too affectionate.

NEKAYA: It really does unsettle us.

GOLD.: Are you really under the impression that English girls are so ridiculously demure? Why, an English girl of the highest type is the best, the most beautiful, the bravest, and the brightest creature that Heaven has conferred upon this world of ours. She is frank, open-hearted, and fearless, and never shows in so favorable a light as when she gives her own blameless impulses full play!

NEKAYA AND KALYBA: Oh, you shocking story!

GOLD.: Not at all. I'm speaking the strict truth. I'll tell you all about her.

SONG—Mr. Goldbury.

A wonderful joy our eyes to bless,
In her magnificent comeliness,
Is an English girl of eleven stone two,
And five foot ten in her dancing shoe!
    She follows the hounds, and on the pounds—
        The "field" tails off and the muffs diminish—

Over the hedges and brooks she bounds,
    Straight as a crow, from find to finish.
At cricket, her kin will lose or win—
    She and her maids, on grass and clover,
Eleven maids out—eleven maids in—
    And perhaps an occasional "maiden over!"

Go search the world and search the sea,
Then come you home and sing with me
There's no such gold and no such pearl
As a bright and beautiful English girl!
With a ten-mile spin she stretches her limbs,
She golfs, she punts, she rows, she swims—
She plays, she sings, she dances, too,
From ten or eleven til all is blue!
  At ball or drum, til small hours come
    (*Chaperon's fans concealing her yawning*)
  She'll waltz away like a teetotum.
    And never go home til daylight's dawning.
  Lawn-tennis may share her favours fair—
    Her eyes a-dance, and her cheeks a-glowing—
  Down comes her hair, but then what does she care?
    It's all her own and it's worth the showing!
      Go search the world, etc.

Her soul is sweet as the ocean air,
For prudery knows no haven there;
To find mock-modesty, please apply
To the conscious blush and the downcast eye.
  Rich in the things contentment brings,
    In every pure enjoyment wealthy,
  Blithe and beautiful bird she sings,
    For body and mind are hale and healthy.
  Her eyes they thrill with right goodwill—
    Her heart is light as a floating feather—
  As pure and bright as the mountain rill
    That leaps and laughs in the Highland heather!
      Go search the world, etc.

QUARTET.

NEK.: Then I may sing and play?
LORD D.: You may!
KAL.: Then I may laugh and shout?
GOLD.: No doubt!.
NEK.: These maxims you endorse?

LORD D.: Of course!

KAL.: You won't exclaim "Oh fie!"

GOLD.: Not I!

GOLD.: Whatever you are—be that:
    Whatever you say—be true:
        Straightforwardly act—
        Be honest—in fact,
        Be nobody else but you.

LORD D.: Give every answer pat—
    Your character true unfurl;
        And when it is ripe,
        You'll then be a type
        Of a capital English girl.

ALL.: Oh sweet surprise—oh, dear delight,
    To find it undisputed quite,
    All musty, fusty rules despite
    That Art is wrong and Nature right!

NEK.: When happy I,
    With laughter glad
        I'll wake the echoes fairly,
    And only sigh
        When I am sad—
        And that will be but rarely!

KAL.: I'll row and fish,
    And gallop, soon—
        No longer be a prim one—
    And when I wish
        To hum a tune,
        It needn't be a hymn one?

GOLD. AND LORD D.: No, no!
    It needn't be a hymn one!

ALL (*dancing*): Oh, sweet surprise and dear delight
    To find it undisputed quite—
    All musty, fusty rules despite—
    That Art is wrong and Nature right!

(*Dance, and off*)

(*Enter Lady Sophy*)

Recitative—Lady Sophy.

Oh, would some demon power the gift impart
To quell my over-conscientious heart—
Unspeak the oaths that never had been spoken,
And break the vows that never should be broken!

Song—Lady Sophy.

When but a maid of fifteen year,
        Unsought—unplighted—
Short petticoated—and, I fear,
        Still shorter-sighted—
I made a vow, one early spring,
That only to some spotless King
Who proof of blameless life could bring
        I'd be united.
For I had read, not long before,
Of blameless kings in fairy lore,
And thought the race still flourished here—
        Well, well—
    I was a maid of fifteen year!
(*The King enters and overhears this verse*)
    Each morning I pursued my game
        (*An early riser*);
For spotless monarchs I became
        An advertiser:
But all in vain I searched each land,
So, kingless, to my native strand
Returned, a little older, and
        A good deal wiser!

I learnt that spotless King and Prince
Have disappeared some ages since—
Even Paramount's angelic grace—
        Ah me!—
Is but a mask on Nature's face!
(*King comes forward*)

KING: Ah, Lady Sophy—then you love me!
    For so you sing—
LADY S.: (*Indignant and surprise. Producing "Palace Peeper"*)
    No, by the stars that shine above me,
        Degraded King!
  For while these rumours, through the city bruited,
  Remain uncontradicted, unrefuted,
  The object thou of my aversion rooted,
      Repulsive thing!
KING: Be just—the time is now at hand
    When truth may published be.
  These paragraphs were written and
    Contributed by me!
LADY S.: By you? No, no!
KING: Yes, yes. I swear, by me!
  I, caught in Scaphio's ruthless toil,
    Contributed the lot!
LADY S.: That that is why you did not boil
    The author on the spot!
KING: And that is why I did not boil
    The author on the spot!
LADY S.: I couldn't think why you did not boil!
KING: But I know why I did not boil
    The author on the spot!

DUET—Lady Sophy and King.

LADY S.: Oh, the rapture unrestrained
    Of a candid retractation!
  For my sovereign has deigned
    A convincing explanation—
  And the clouds that gathered o'er
    All have vanished in the distance,
  And the Kings of fairy lore
    One, at least, is in existence!
KING: Oh, the skies are blue above,
    And the earth is red and rosal,
  Now the lady of my love
    Has accepted my proposal!

For that asinorum pons
  I have crossed without assistance,
And of prudish paragons
  One, at least, is in existence!
(*King and Lady Sophy dance gracefully. While this is going on Lord Dramaleigh enters unobserved with Nekaya and Capt. Fitzbattleaxe. The two girls direct Zara's attention to the King and Lady Sophy, who are still dancing affectionately together. At this point the King kisses Lady Sophy, which causes the Princesses to make an exclamation. The King and Lady Sophy are at first much confused at being detected, but eventually throw off all reserve, and the four couples break into a wild Tarantella, and at the end exeunt severally*)
Enter all the male Chorus, in great excitement, for various entrances, led by Scaphio, Phantis, and Tarara, and followed by the female Chorus.

CHORUS.

Upon our sea-girt land
At our enforced command
Reform has laid her hand
    Like some remorseless ogress—
And made us darkly rue
The deeds she dared to do—
And all is owing to
    Those hated Flowers of Progress!

So down with them!
So down with them!
Reform's a hated ogress.
    So down with them!
    So down with them!
Down with the Flowers of Progress!
(*Flourish. Enter King, his three daughters, Lady Sophy, and the Flowers of Progress*)
KING: What means this most unmannerly irruption?
    Is this your gratitude for boons conferred?
SCAPHIO: Boons? Bah! A fico for such boons, say we!
    These boons have brought Utopia to a standstill!
    Our pride and boast—the Army and the Navy—
    Have both been reconstructed and remodeled

Upon so irresistible a basis
That all the neighboring nations have disarmed—
And War's impossible! Your County Councillor
Has passed such drastic Sanitary laws
That all doctors dwindle, starve, and die!
The laws, remodeled by Sir Bailey Barre,
Have quite extinguished crime and litigation:
The lawyers starve, and all the jails are let
As model lodgings for the working-classes!
In short—Utopia, swamped by dull Prosperity, Demands that
    these detested Flowers of Progress
Be sent about their business, and affairs
Restored to their original complexion!

KING: (*to Zara*) My daughter, this is a very unpleasant state of things. What is to be done?

ZARA: I don't know—I don't understand it. We must have omitted something.

KING: Omitted something? Yes, that's all very well, but—(*Sir Bailey Barre whispers to Zara.*)

ZARA: (*suddenly*) Of course! Now I remember! Why, I had forgotten the most essential element of all!

KING: And that is?—

ZARA: Government by Party! Introduce that great and glorious element—at once the bulwark and foundation of England's greatness—and all will be well! No political measures will endure, because one Party will assuredly undo all that the other Party has done; and while grouse is to be shot, and foxes worried to death, the legislative action of the country will be at a standstill. Then there will be sickness in plenty, endless lawsuits, crowded jails, interminable confusion in the Army and Navy, and, in short, general and unexampled prosperity!

ALL: Ulahlica! Ulahlica!

PHANTIS: (*aside*) Baffled!

SCAPHIO: But an hour will come!

KING: Your hour has come already—away with them, and let them wait my will! (*Scaphio and Phantis are led off in custody*) From this moment Government by Party is adopted, with all its attendant blessings; and henceforward Utopia will no longer be a Monarchy Limited, but, what is a great deal better, a Limited Monarchy!

FINALE.

ZARA: There's a little group of isles beyond the wave—
    So tiny, you might almost wonder where it is—
That nation is the bravest of the brave,
    And cowards are the rarest of all rarities.
The proudest nations kneel at her command;
    She terrifies all foreign-born rapscallions;
And holds the peace of Europe in her hand
    With half a score invincible battalions!

    Such, at least, is the tale
        Which is born on the gale,
    From the island which dwells in the sea.
        Let us hope, for her sake
    That she makes no mistake—
        That she's all the professes to be!
KING: Oh, may we copy all her maxims wise,
    And imitate her virtues and her charities;
And may we, by degrees, acclimatize
    Her Parliamentary peculiarities!
By doing so, we shall in course of time,
    Regenerate completely our entire land—
Great Britain is the monarchy sublime,
    To which some add (*others do not*) Ireland.
    Such at least is the tale, etc.

CURTAIN

A Note About the Authors

Arthur Sullivan (1842–1900) and W.S. Gilbert (1836–1911) were theatrical collaborators during the nineteenth century. Prior to their partnership, Gilbert wrote and illustrated stories as a child, eventually developing his signature "topsy-turvy" style. Sullivan was raised in a musical family where he learned to play multiple instruments at an early age. Together, their talents would help produce a successful series of comic operas. Some notable titles include *The Pirates of Penzance*, *The Sorcerer*, *H.M.S. Pinafore*, and *The Mikado*.

A Note from the Publisher

Spanning many genres, from non-fiction essays to literature classics to children's books and lyric poetry, Mint Edition books showcase the master works of our time in a modern new package. The text is freshly typeset, is clean and easy to read, and features a new note about the author in each volume. Many books also include exclusive new introductory material. Every book boasts a striking new cover, which makes it as appropriate for collecting as it is for gift giving. Mint Edition books are only printed when a reader orders them, so natural resources are not wasted. We're proud that our books are never manufactured in excess and exist only in the exact quantity they need to be read and enjoyed.

.

bookfinity™

Discover more of your favorite classics with Bookfinity™.

- Track your reading with custom book lists.
- Get great book recommendations for your personalized Reader Type.
- Add reviews for your favorite books.
- AND MUCH MORE!

Visit **bookfinity.com** and take the fun Reader Type quiz to get started.

Enjoy our classic and modern companion pairings!

Classic & Modern

Bookfinity is a registered trademark of Ingram Book Group LLC. © 2023 Bookfinity. All rights reserved.

www.ingramcontent.com/pod-product-compliance
Lightning Source LLC
Chambersburg PA
CBHW020605030426
42337CB00013B/1220